YOU'RE ALREADY A SUCCESS!
BY PEGGY BALLARD

**THOUGHTS
ON BEGINNING
YOUR NEW
CAREER**

**Andrews McMeel
Publishing**

Kansas City

00 01 02 03 04 RDC 10 9 8 7 6 5 4 3 2 1

Library of Congress Cataloging-in-Publication Data

Ballard, Peggy.
   You're already a success : thoughts on beginning your new career /
   Peggy. Ballard.
      p. cm.
   ISBN 0-7407-0466-4
      1. Vocational guidance. 2. Success in business. I. Title.

HF5381 .B245 2000
650.1—dc21   99-57368
                                                                CIP

Book design and composition by Lisa Martin
Illustrations by Matthew Taylor

To the best of the author's knowledge, all quotes are stated accurately and original authors have been properly credited. If notified, the publisher will be pleased to rectify an error in future editions.

This book is dedicated to my parents,
who gave me my faith in God,
and, therefore, my courage.

And to my husband, Greg,
who gives me love and laughter.

INTRODUCTION

This book was originally a Christmas present for my niece Laura Cobb. A senior at Clemson University, she had just accepted an internship in the marketing department at Delta Air Lines. Her career was just beginning, while I had been in the workplace for more than twenty years. When I started this book, my goal was to give Laura a head start on learning some of the keys to success and career satisfaction that I have learned along the way. I wanted her to know that she was already a success—no matter what job she held.

I have been fortunate in my career. I went from being a southern woman from a typical southern town to a career woman who lived in Atlanta, Georgia, then San Francisco, New York City, and London before landing back in Atlanta. I've gone from being a teacher to a secretary to vice president at a major high-technology company—all without a mentor to coach me. I wanted Laura to have a mentor to carry with her to work.

This book contains "quick thoughts" on how to succeed when you are at a transition point in your life, whether you are just out of school and walking into the workplace for the first time or changing direction in your career and taking on new responsibilities.

Laura and I share this book with you along with our hope that it will encourage you to expand your self-confidence and maximize your potential. You have much to offer the world. Like most people, all you need are words of encouragement and a little guidance now and then.

Use this book as your starter to take some of the mystery out of what to expect as you begin your new career. Trust yourself and learn from your experiences, both good and bad. And, most important, remember . . . you're already a success . . . no matter what!

Peggy Ballard

OWNING YOUR OWN POWER

Too often people begin a new job taking a backseat. You may think that you are too young or too inexperienced. You may be timid in your approach to work. You don't own your own power.

You can find satisfaction and success in your work by seizing the opportunities presented to you. Satisfaction comes from knowing that you are being true to yourself. Speaking out. Knowing what you want. Standing up for what you think and believe. Being your powerful self.

Think of yourself as an equal. And take actions to show that you are. Only you can be responsible for you . . . and to do so, you must own your own power.

"If there is faith that can move mountains,
it is faith in your own power."

—MARIE VON EBNER-ESCHENBACH
(late eighteenth-century–early nineteenth-century Austrian author)

Believe in yourself.

"To accomplish great things,

we must not only act,

but also dream;

not only plan

but also believe."

—ANATOLE FRANCE
(nineteenth-century French author)

Remember:

Personally, you may be younger . . .
Professionally, you're the same age:

ADULT

*"Never tell a young person that anything cannot be done.
God may have been waiting centuries for someone
ignorant enough of the impossible to do that very thing."*

—JOHN ANDREW HOLMES
(contemporary American author)

ATTITUDE
IS THE KEY TO SUCCESS.

*"Things turn out best for the people who
make the best of the way things turn out."*

—JOHN WOODEN
(former UCLA basketball coach)

*"You have to be taught to be second class;
you're not born that way."*

—LENA HORNE
(contemporary American singer)

*"The greatest discovery of my generation is that human
beings can alter their lives by altering their attitudes of mind."*

—WILLIAM JAMES
(late nineteenth-century philosopher)

*"Unless you choose to do great things with it,
it makes no difference how much you are rewarded,
or how much power you have."*

—OPRAH WINFREY
(contemporary American talk
show host, entertainer, producer)

LOOK PEOPLE
IN THE EYE.

Connect.

Don't wait for the other person

to extend their hand.

EXTEND yours first and

shake hands FIRMLY.

INTRODUCE
YOURSELF.

Call people by their names.

"Really big people are,
   above **everything** else,
courteous, considerate, and *generous*—
   not just to some people
in some circumstances—
   but to **everyone** all the time."

—THOMAS J. WATSON (founder of IBM)

When answering the phone, say your full name . . .

"This is Laura Cobb."

When calling someone, identify yourself—

> *"This is Laura Cobb of Edelman Public Relations. May I speak with Peggy Ballard?"*

Drop the
"Yes, Ma'am" and "Yes, Sir."

Don't call women
"girls," "gals," or "ladies."

VALUE your opinion

and **OFFER** it.

*"The difference between 'involvement'
and 'commitment' is like an eggs-and-ham
breakfast: The chicken was 'involved'—
the pig was 'committed.'"*

—AUTHOR UNKNOWN

Be confident.

"With confidence, you can reach truly
amazing heights; without confidence,
even the simplest accomplishments are
beyond your grasp."

—JIM LOEHR
(contemporary American businessman)

Don't worry. Plan instead.

"Let your advance worrying become
advanced thinking and planning."

—WINSTON CHURCHILL
(former British prime minister and statesman)

Don't be a people pleaser.

PLEASE YOURSELF.

"I don't know the key to success,
but the key to failure is
trying to please everyone."

—BILL COSBY
(contemporary American
entertainer, author, TV producer)

Be conservative in your dress
but don't be dull.

Women can wear the same outfit
twice in a week. **Men do.**

*"Dress and conduct yourself so that people who have
been in your company will not recall what you had on."*

—JOHN NEWTON
(English pastor, author, hymn writer;
author of *Amazing Grace*)

BE DECISIVE.

Take action.

"Even if you're on the right track,
you'll get run over if you just sit there."

—WILL ROGERS
(twentieth-century American
cowboy actor and humorist)

You will make mistakes . . .

Just own up to them.

"Good judgment comes from experience,
and experience—well,
that comes from poor judgment."

—AUTHOR UNKNOWN

"NO."
is a complete sentence.

"I DON'T KNOW"

is an acceptable answer . . .

particularly when

you don't know.

FIND THE ANSWER.

Your **ROAD** to success is a *journey* of *communications*.

Learn to *write well* and become a **STRONG** presenter.

"I see work on communication not as the acquisition of some specific skill but as a journey, a journey that helps individuals explore and express more of themselves, both as businesspeople and as human beings."

—SANDY LINVER
(president of Speakeasy Inc.; from *The Leader's Edge*)

Most important . . .

Enjoy the powerful YOU!

Know . . .

you *can* make it on your own.

*"Opportunity dances with those
who are already on the dance floor."*

—H. JACKSON BROWN JR.
(contemporary American author)

GETTING ALONG

Your ability to get along in business is directly related to your ability to get along with people. How you meet people, treat people, and lead people will make a difference in your success at work. Don't think that you have to change your personality or need to become a "people person" to get along in business. Just remember the Golden Rule—"Do unto others."

Be yourself.

Share yourself.

"The valuable person in any business is the individual who can and will cooperate with others."

—Elbert Hubbard
(American writer)

Be interested—
not interesting.

"The secret of being a bore is to tell everything."

—VOLTAIRE
(French satirist, philosopher, historian)

22

Make your boss look good.

Make your coworkers look good.

You'll *really* look good!

*"Individuals play the game,
but teams win championships."*

—Author unknown

Meet new people.

Welcome them into the
company and the department.

*"Don't wait for people to be friendly,
show them how."*

—Author unknown

Don't complain.

Keep confidences.

Don't gossip.

*"Great minds discuss ideas,
average minds discuss events,
small minds discuss people."*

—HYMAN G. RICKOVER
(admiral, U.S. Navy)

REMEMBER
YOUR
INTEGRITY.

"To be persuasive, we must be believable;
To be believable, we must be credible;
To be credible, we must be truthful."

—EDWARD R. MURROW (American journalist)

Listen.

Wait for other people to
   complete what they're saying
before you speak.

*"The greatest gift you can give
another is the purity of your attention."*

—RICHARD MOSS
(contemporary American author and teacher)

Believe in others.

Treat everyone as a mentor.

You can learn from everyone.

"This I do believe above all,
especially in my times of greater discouragement,
that I must believe—that I must believe in
my fellow men—that I must believe in myself—
and I must believe in God—
if life is to have any meaning."

—MARGARET CHASE SMITH
(twentieth-century American
congresswoman and senator)

Encourage people.

Congratulate people.

**Celebrate successes—
no matter whose
or how small.**

"He who obtains has little.
He who scatters has much."

—LAO-TZU
(Chinese general and
philosopher, 604–531 B.C.)

Most important,

be yourself . . .

You're already a success.

"You are wholly complete and your success in life
will be in direct proportion to your ability
to accept this truth about you."

—DR. ROBERT ANTHONY
(contemporary American author)

TOOLS OF
THE TRADE

In any job, you will find certain "tools" that will assist you in your success. Knowledge can be a tool—just as a computer, voice mail, and planning are tools. The more you can learn about your company's business, its customers, products and services, and business in general, the more valuable you will be to your company and the more rewarding your job will become.

As you begin your new career, be observant. Notice what makes you tick and what helps you "run" your business life. And look for new things to learn wherever and whenever you can.

Know your company's

VISION,

MISSION, and

QUALITY POLICY.

Make them your own.

Know your company's
products and services.

Know your customers—

INTERNAL

and EXTERNAL.

When giving a presentation, or writing
a letter or report . . .

know your audience.

When traveling . . .

pack *lightly,*

tip **HEAVILY**.

A hotel concierge is
a valuable resource.

Brainstorm.

BE CREATIVE.

Generate ideas.

BOUNCE

ideas off of colleagues.

*"I not only use all the brains I have,
but all I can borrow."*

—WOODROW WILSON
(twenty-eighth president of the United States)

Read:

The local newspaper

The *Wall Street Journal*

Industry publications

Books on business

Books for fun

JUST READ.

"Reading is to the mind what exercise is to the body."

—JOSEPH ADDISON
(late seventeenth-century
English essayist, humorist, poet)

Set objectives.

"In the long run, men hit only what they aim at."

—HENRY DAVID THOREAU
(nineteenth-century American author and social critic)

Set deadlines.

"Someday is not a day of the week."

—AUTHOR UNKNOWN

Measure your results.

"In business, words are words;
explanations are explanations;
promises are promises;
but only performance is reality."

—HAROLD GENEEN
(former chairman of ITT and author of *The Synergy Myth*)

37

Plan:

Your day

Your projects

Your presentations

Questions that you want to ask

Questions that might be asked of you

JUST PLAN.

Keep a journal . . .

You never know when you'll need to
update your résumé or write your
performance appraisal or job description.

Develop a portfolio . . .

You'll create work that you will be proud
of for the rest of your life.

BE COMPUTER LITERATE.

Know how to surf the Web.
Know how to use E-mail and
Microsoft Word, PowerPoint, and Excel.
Always spell-check.

*"When you turn on the television, you close your mind.
When you turn on your computer, you open it."*

—BILL GATES
(founder, Microsoft Corporation)

Answer your own telephone.

Use voice mail,
but don't hide behind it.

When you're out of the office,
change your voice mail to let callers
know when you'll be back.

Return phone calls **promptly**.

41

COLLECT BUSINESS CARDS.

Make notes to yourself on the back, reminding yourself of when and where you met and any other pertinent information.

"It is singular how soon we lose the impression of what ceases to be constantly before us."

—LORD BYRON (nineteenth-century English poet)

When you call a meeting,
lead the meeting:

SET objectives.

CREATE an agenda.

FOLLOW the agenda.

Summarize actions and decisions.

End on time.

It pays to be early . . .

- to work

- to a meeting

- when meeting your deadlines.

"The secret of your future is hidden
in your daily routine."

—MIKE MURDOCK
(contemporary American minister and writer)

FOCUS.

Set priorities.

*"If you chase two rabbits,
both will escape."*

—AUTHOR UNKNOWN

45

When you get overwhelmed with your
work load . . .

Remember:

Climb the mountain

ONE STEP

AT A TIME.

"Mountains cannot be surmounted except by winding paths."

—JOHANN WOLFGANG VON GOETHE
(late eighteenth-century–early
nineteenth-century German author)

Your manager's success

depends on your success.

Don't be afraid to ask your manager

for guidance or help.

*"It's the men behind
who 'make' the men ahead."*

—MERLE CROWELL
(twentieth-century American writer)

47

Take pride in all you do . . .

"Care more than others think is wise,
Risk more than others think is safe,
Dream more than others think is practical,
Expect more than others think is possible!"

—AUTHOR UNKNOWN

THE BOTTOM LINE

While you may choose a marketing, sales, or engineering career, finance will always play a role in your work. To be successful you must be able to read and understand the financial side of business—no matter how much you dislike numbers.

And, from a personal point of view, you need to make sure that all of your hard work does not go to waste. Make sure that you have something financially to show for your success.

Know the financial lingo:

PBT (Profit Before Taxes)

ROI (Return On Investments)

ABOVE THE LINE

BELOW THE LINE

Cost of goods

Read and understand your company's
annual report.

Be able to answer:

"What were your company's sales revenues . . .

for the past year?

the past quarter?"

Ask your boss

to explain to you

your department's

budget.

Understand your role

in the company's

bottom line.

You'll find it easier to do your expense report if you keep your business expenses separate from personal expenses.

Don't spend your expense check reimbursement for personal expenses.

Take a financial planning course.

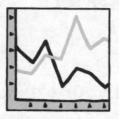

Understand stock options.

Start saving for a house—

NOW!

Start saving for retirement—

NOW!

Participate in your company's 401(k) program.

Put $2,000 in an IRA each year.

*"You can be young without money,
but you can't be old without it."*

—TENNESSEE WILLIAMS
(American playwright and novelist)

When you get a raise, increase your savings.

"It is no use to wait for your ship to come in
unless you have sent one out."

—AUTHOR UNKNOWN

Don't charge—but if you do,

pay off the balance

each month.

Don't get into debt.

"Debt is the worst poverty."

—THOMAS FULLER
(seventeenth-century English cleric)

Always know your market value.

What do other people in
similar positions make?

Don't be afraid to ask for
a salary worth your value.

*"A bar of iron costs $5, made into horseshoes
its worth is $12, made into needles its worth is
$3,500, made into balance springs for watches,
its worth is $300,000. Your own value is determined
also by what you are able to make of yourself."*

—AUTHOR UNKNOWN

Believe it or not . . . .

numbers can be

your friends.

MOVING UP

Whenever you start a new job, make sure that you have an idea of what you want your next job to be. Dream. Think big. Exceed your expectations.

Take actions that will take you to that next job. Every job is an opportunity for advancement. Believe in your success.

"Making a success

of the job at hand

is the best step toward

the kind you want."

—BERNARD M. BARUCH
(twentieth-century American statesman)

**Starting at the bottom is fine as long as you
point yourself in the right direction.**

Be able to recognize your company's

executives in a crowd—

especially the president or CEO . . .

and your boss's boss.

EXCEED EXPECTATIONS.

Don't be satisfied
with mediocrity.

*"The unreasonable man tries to change
the world around him. The reasonable
man adapts to the world around him.
Therefore, all progress depends
on the unreasonable man."*

—GEORGE BERNARD SHAW
(Irish-born British playwright)

Take advantage of the training
your company has to offer.

Think about getting your master's degree.
(If your company offers an educational
program, pursue an advanced degree.)

"Education's purpose
is to replace an empty mind
with an open one."

—MALCOLM FORBES
(twentieth-century publisher and sportsman)

64

See something that needs to be done?

DO IT.

"There's a fine line between
   fishing and standing
on the shore
      like an idiot."

—STEVEN WRIGHT
(contemporary American comedian)

BE FLEXIBLE.

EXPECT CHANGE.

"I can't change the direction of the wind, but I can adjust my sails to always reach my destination."

—JIMMY DEAN
(contemporary American entertainer)

Don't be afraid to
   leave a job or make a change—

JUMP.

But make sure that you're
   not just **running** away.

*"We cannot become what we need to be,
   remaining what we are."*

—MAX DEPREE
(chairman and CEO, Herman Miller, Inc.)

Know the signs that say it is time to move on in a job:

- Your company's financial status is in jeopardy.

- Your position in the company is no longer secure.

- You feel bored more often than you feel challenged.

- You're not having fun anymore.

*"Courage is the power to
let go of the familiar."*

—MARY BRYANT
(contemporary American model
and motivational speaker)

Keep your desk and office neat and clean.

Keep your car clean.
(You never know when you'll have
to drive your boss to lunch.)

Polish your shoes.

Start the day early.

Use the quiet time in the office to "think outside the box."

"Thoughts are energy.

You can make your world

or break your world

by thinking."

—SUSAN TAYLOR
(contemporary American
journalist and editor)

Ask "What do I need
to be doing differently?"

BE OPEN
TO FEEDBACK.

*"He who stops being better
stops being good."*

—OLIVER CROMWELL
(Lord Protector of England, seventeenth century)

YOU'RE
ALREADY
A
SUCCESS

IMAGINE

THE

BEST

and . . .

"Never, never, never give up."

—Winston Churchill
(former British prime minister and statesman)

TAKING CARE OF YOU

No matter how important success in a career may be to you, a job means nothing if you aren't enjoying life. To be successful, you must have a balance in life. And, you will soon find out, life is a balancing act.

"There are two things to aim at in life: first, to get what you want, and after that, to enjoy it. Only the wisest of mankind achieve the second."

—LOGAN PEARSALL SMITH
(American essayist)

Trust yourself.

Always stand up for your

values and *beliefs*—

at work and at play.

*"Character is much easier
kept than recovered."*

—THOMAS PAINE
(late seventeenth-century English-born
American Revolutionary War patriot and author)

Take time for lunch.

TAKE A WALK.

TAKE A BREATHER.

 LAUGH.

"The most wasted day of all is that on which we have not laughed."

—SÉBASTIEN ROCH NICOLAS CHAMFORT
(eighteenth-century French writer)

75

Don't take work home—

unless you're really going to do the work.

You'll wake up in the morning
feeling guilty that you didn't
do it.

PRAY OR MEDITATE.

Ask for guidance.

You'll get answers.

(Often, later than you would like . . .
and often not the answers you expect!)

JUST BE
PATIENT.

At times you will find yourself afraid.

Don't let it stop you.

Keep going.

The fear doesn't last forever.

"Most of our obstacles would melt away if,
instead of cowering before them,
we should make up our minds to
walk boldly through them."

—ORISON SWETT MARDEN
(contemporary motivational author)

Take risks . . .

- Travel

- Move to a new city

- Change jobs

- Ask for a raise

*"And the trouble is,
if you don't risk anything,
you risk even more."*

—ERICA JONG
(American writer)

Own a passport.

*"A man should ever be ready
booted to take his journey."*

—MICHEL EYQUEM DE MONTAIGNE
(sixteenth-century French essayist)

Give to charity and

your community.

Donate your time

and your money.

*"We make a living by what we get,
we make a life by what we give."*

—WINSTON CHURCHILL
(former British prime minister and statesman)

KEEP UP
WITH OLD FRIENDS.

They are full of old memories
and treasures that will bring you
laughter and delight.

*"To let a friendship die away by
negligence and silence is certainly
not wise. It is voluntarily to throw
away one of the greatest comforts
of the weary pilgrimage."*

—SAMUEL JOHNSON
(eighteenth-century English writer)

Think of your family.

Remember

BIRTHDAYS,

ANNIVERSARIES,

HOLIDAYS.

Call. Write. Send E-mails.

*"Other things may change us,
but we start and end with family."*

—Anthony Brandt
(contemporary American writer)

Don't let your imagination
take over what is real.

Say to yourself

"I'm smart."

"I'm doing a great job."

"I look great."

"I have much to offer."

"I deserve good things in life."

+

TAKING
CARE
OF YOU

HAVE OUTSIDE
INTERESTS AND HOBBIES.

Your job isn't your life . . .

you are your life.

"Few people do business well
who do nothing else."

—PHILIP DORMER STANHOPE CHESTERFIELD
(English statesman and author)

85

Exercise.

"After thirty, a body
has a mind of its own."

—BETTE MIDLER
(contemporary American singer and actor)

Pets bring

fun *and*

love

into your life.

Write down your goals. Share them with a friend.

Even if you don't create an elaborate plan to reach those goals, you'll have a direction and you'll surprise yourself when you reach your goal. Your declaration in the written word has power.

*"We should all be concerned about the future
because we will have to spend the
rest of our lives there."*

—CHARLES F. KETTERING
(American engineer and inventor)

Don't take work too seriously.

Don't take yourself too seriously.

"You will do foolish things, but do them with enthusiasm."

—COLETTE
(French writer)

Look for the truth in the negative
and learn from it—
But focus on the positive.

Remember . . .

no matter what job

you have in life,

you're already a success.

ENJOY LIFE.
MAKE A DIFFERENCE.

*"Even if I knew that tomorrow the world would go to
pieces, I would still plant my apple tree."*

—DR. MARTIN LUTHER KING JR.
(African-American clergyman and civil rights leader)

RESOURCES

Here's a sampling of Internet sites and books that I have found very helpful. Why not try a few? . . . Also, check out my Web site at **www.quickthoughts.com** for a list of more resources. While you are there, be sure to give me your feedback and let me hear how you're succeeding.

www.socojoblink.org/selftst2.htm

This site contains links to several self-tests that can help you determine general career interests and personality traits as they relate to work.

www.monster.com

In addition to more than 200,000 job listings, this site includes career-related feature articles and a career resources center with information tailored to various careers and career stages.

www.businessweek.com

A Web site full of helpful information from what's going on in the global business marketplace to careers.

www.careers.com

Go to this site for career listings, salary information, and job aptitude testing.

How to Be a Star at Work: Nine Breakthrough Strategies You Need to Succeed, Robert E. Kelley, Times Business, Random House, New York, 1999.

Like most people, you probably think that star performers are smarter, more creative, more outgoing, are risk takers, and have more drive. Not so says the research. Interesting reading and you will learn that "A star isn't born—a star is made . . . and you can make yourself into a star." Good, commonsense information and food for thought.

Women in Power: The Secrets of Leadership, Dorothy W. Cantor and Toni Bernay, Houghton Mifflin, New York, 1992.

This book will give you insight into the powerful women in a mostly male society—American politics. You'll read interviews with twenty-five of the most influential women in politics and learn the secrets that gave them the confidence to take on the status quo.

Feel the Fear and Do It Anyway, Susan Jeffers, Ph.D., Fawcctt Columbine, New York, 1987.

This book has stood the test of time. Too often we let our fears and our mind's negative chatter stop us from growing. This book will make you realize when you are feeling powerless and give you the tools to do something about it. A must-read.

Speak Easy, Speak and Get Results, and *The Leader's Edge*
Three books by Sandy Linver, founder and president of Speakeasy, a communications consulting company with offices in Atlanta and San Francisco. Since 1974 Speakeasy has been helping people reach their full potential through more effective communication. I recommend that you do whatever it takes to attend one of Speakeasy's work-shops offered weekly. (Call 404/261-4029 in Atlanta or check out their Web site at www.speakeasyinc.com.)